If I Were a
Firefighter

by Thomas Kingsley Troupe   illustrated by Mick Reid

Special thanks to our adviser for his expertise:

Terry Flaherty, Ph.D.
Professor of English
Minnesota State University, Mankato

PICTURE WINDOW BOOKS
a capstone imprint

This book is dedicated to the brave men and women of the Woodbury Fire Department.
I'm proud to count myself among your ranks.—TKT

Editors: Shelly Lyons and Jennifer Besel
Designer: Tracy Davies
Art Director: Nathan Gassman
Production Specialist: Jane Klenk

The illustrations in this book were created with watercolor and colored pencil.

Picture Window Books
151 Good Counsel Drive
P.O. Box 669
Mankato, MN 56002-0669
877-845-8392
www.picturewindowbooks.com

Printed in the United States of America in North Mankato, Minnesota.

092009
005618CGS10

Library of Congress Cataloging-in-Publication Data
Troupe, Thomas Kingsley.
If I were a firefighter / by Thomas Kingsley Troupe ; illustrated by
Mick Reid.
p. cm. — (Dream big!)
Includes index.
ISBN 978-1-4048-5535-9 (library binding)
1. Fire extinction—Juvenile literature. 2. Fire fighters—Juvenile
literature. I. Reid, Mick, ill. II. Title.
TH9148.T75 2010
628.9'25—dc22   2009024067

If I were a firefighter, I would save people and their houses from fire.

If I were a firefighter, I would be ready for any emergency. Some nights I would sleep at the fire station. The fire alarm would ring!

Clang! Clang! Clang!

6

If I were a firefighter, I would slide down the pole. The fire trucks would be waiting downstairs. I would jump into my boots and pull up my fire pants. I would slip into my heavy fire coat, helmet, mask, and gloves.

A firefighter wears "turnout," or "bunker," gear. This heavy clothing has thick layers to keep out heat. The helmet's face shield keeps dangerous matter away from the firefighter's eyes, nose, and mouth.

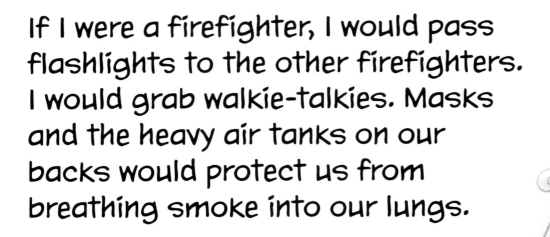

If I were a firefighter, I would pass flashlights to the other firefighters. I would grab walkie-talkies. Masks and the heavy air tanks on our backs would protect us from breathing smoke into our lungs.

Let's go!

Firefighters sit behind the truck driver in a place called the "dog house."

9

If I were a firefighter, I would drive the fire truck. We would race through streets with our lights flashing. The loud sirens and horns would tell cars to move out of our way.

HONK! HONK! Honk!

If I were a firefighter, I would park the fire truck near a fire hydrant. I would connect the big hose to the hydrant. The hydrant would fill our pumper truck with water.

Whoosh!

There are different kinds of fire trucks. A ladder truck can raise a long ladder to reach high places. A pumper truck has a large tank filled with water and foam.

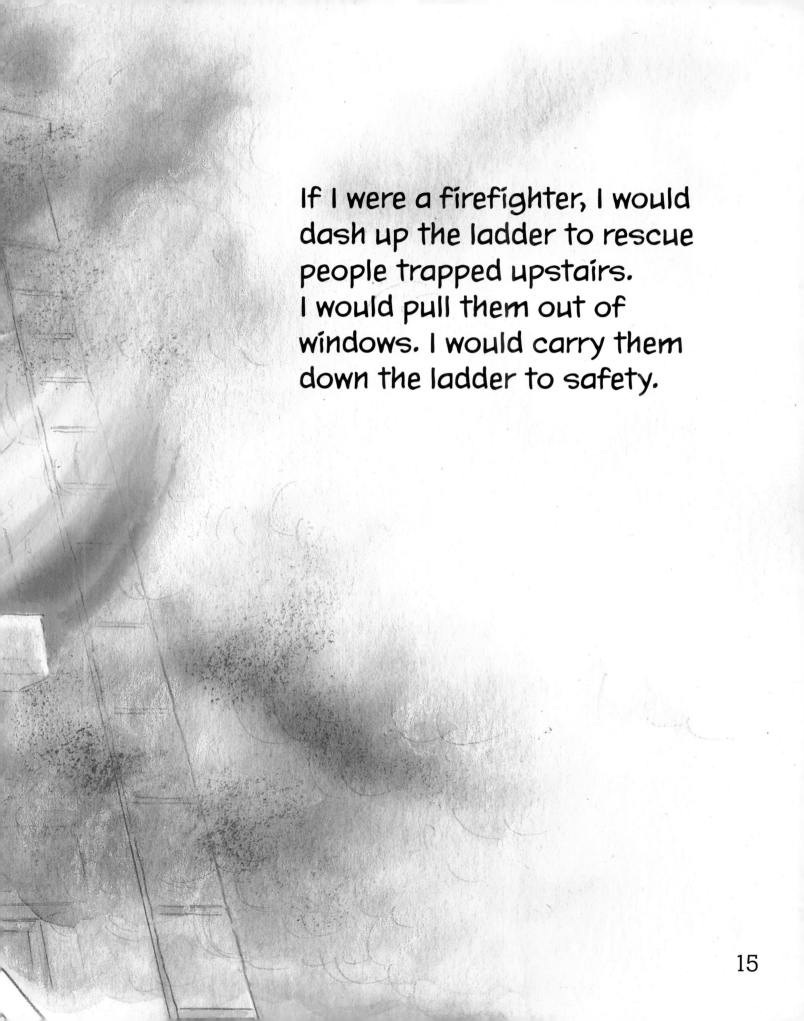

If I were a firefighter, I would dash up the ladder to rescue people trapped upstairs. I would pull them out of windows. I would carry them down the ladder to safety.

If I were a firefighter, I would chop through doors with an axe to get inside the burning house. I would rush in and blast the flames with water and foam.

Hisssss!

If I were a firefighter, I would always be ready for another fire.

Clang! Clang! Clang!

Here we go again!

Being a firefighter would be a dangerous job. Many people would look to me to save them and their homes from fire. It would be nice to feel like a hero!

How do you get to be a Firefighter?

Men and women who want to be firefighters go to classes. They learn all about different kinds of fire. They learn how lots of things burn. They also learn how to put out fires with water and special foam. They practice using axes, hose nozzles, and other tools. They also learn how to break locks and cut off car doors. Special classes teach firefighters how to use the pumps inside the fire truck, as well as drive to fire scenes quickly and safely.

Firefighters need to eat well and exercise regularly. The fire gear and tools they carry can weigh up to 45 pounds (20.3 kilograms). It's also very hot inside the clothing, even before the firefighters get into the burning house. An average firefighter can lose about 5 pounds (2.3 kg) during a large fire, just from the exercise of putting out the fire.

Being a firefighter is a challenging and exciting career. But it is also truly rewarding.

Glossary

emergency—when people are in need of help quickly

fire hydrant—a pipe that sticks up from the ground; fire trucks connect to them to fill their hoses with water.

foam—a special mixture of chemicals and water used to quickly put out fires

gear—items firefighters use to fight fires, including clothing, tools, and hoses

mask—a piece of gear that covers a firefighter's face; it can be hooked up to an air tank to help a firefighter breathe.

pump—the machine inside a fire truck that pulls water into the fire truck and fills the hoses the firefighters use

rescue—to save from danger

To Learn More

More Books to Read

Bingham, Caroline. *Fire Truck.* New York: DK Publishing, 2003.

Demarest, Chris L. *Hotshots!* New York: Margaret K. McElderry, 2003.

Dubois, Muriel L. *Out and About at the Fire Station.* Minneapolis: Picture Window Books, 2003.

Hoena, B. A. *The Fire Station.* Mankato, Minn.: Capstone Press, 2004.

Internet Sites

FactHound offers a safe, fun way to find Internet sites related to this book. All of the sites on FactHound have been researched by our staff.

Here's all you do:

Visit *www.facthound.com*

FactHound will fetch the best sites for you!

Index

Look for all of the books in the Dream Big! series:

If I Were a Ballerina
If I Were a Cowboy
If I Were a Firefighter
If I Were a Major League Baseball Player
If I Were an Astronaut
If I Were the President